Original title:
Tumbleweed Tales

Copyright © 2025 Creative Arts Management OÜ
All rights reserved.

Author: Ophelia Ravenscroft
ISBN HARDBACK: 978-1-80566-681-3
ISBN PAPERBACK: 978-1-80566-966-1

Mirage of the Mind

A cactus dances, oh so spry,
With shadows flicking, passing by.
I squint to see a drink so clear,
But it's just a mirage, that much is near.

A funny hat atop my head,
With visions of a loaf of bread.
In breezy thoughts, my plans unfold,
Yet all I have is dust, I'm told.

Trails of the Unseen

Wander down a winding lane,
Where where the path has gone is plain.
Each twist and turn a giggle brings,
For shadows dance and laughter sings.

Invisible friends join in the jive,
In the dust where daydreams thrive.
I follow footprints, off they go,
To mischief only they can show.

Dusty Footprints

Chasing after footprints, bright and bold,
They giggle as they flee, uncontrolled.
Sneaky grains of sand, oh what a tease,
They swirl around with playful ease.

A tumble here, a trip on air,
I tumble down, not a soul to care.
With every step the laughter grows,
In dusty tales, anything goes.

Secrets of the Sahara

Beneath the sun, the secrets hide,
In dunes so high, they laugh and glide.
Whispers of the wind, they tease,
With silly stories floating with ease.

A mirage waves from the golden sand,
I reach for it, but it slips from hand.
The cacti chuckle, the lizards grin,
As I chase shadows, my fun begins.

The Voyage of the Lost Traveler

A traveler set out on a quest,
His map was a joke, his sense of jest.
He took a wrong turn, and what a sight,
Found a cactus in a tutu, quite the fright!

He asked a squirrel for directions,
The squirrel just laughed, full of affections.
Finding his way wasn't on the cards,
So he danced with a goat in the yards!

With each mile he lost his way,
Came across people who loved to sway.
A party in the desert, no one could see,
But the traveler felt like a VIP!

The sun set low, shadows did waltz,
He learned that it's fun to stumble and fall.
When lost on the road, there's glee to find,
In every misstep, a memory to bind!

Reminiscences from the Dust-choked Road

On a dusty road, stories are weaved,
Of a man who thought he'd achieved.
He packed a lunch but forgot the bread,
Instead, he had twigs and a jam jar, dread!

His bike had a flat; he sat in despair,
A tumbleweed rolled by, without a care.
He knotted his shoes, tried to ride on grass,
But ended up dancing with a cow, alas!

The sun beat down, and he looked quite wild,
Trying to charm a very grumpy child.
With jokes that fell flat like his bicycle tire,
Laughter erupted, igniting the fire!

At dusk, he set camp with dreams in his mind,
And remembered the moments, the ones he'd left behind.
Through bumps and the dust, he'd endlessly roam,
On roads made of laughter, the world's his home!

The Dusty Chronicles

In a town where the dust bunnies play,
A tumble-down sign just runs away,
The old dog laughs, and the cat takes flight,
Chasing dreams in the soft fading light.

A cactus wears sunglasses so bright,
Telling tales of the wild, breezy night,
A rooster who thinks he can really sing,
In harmony with the wind's playful swing.

The wheelbarrow rolls with a quirky cheer,
As the jackrabbit hops, drawing near,
With a wink and a hop, the antics unfold,
In the land of the funny, the brave, and the bold.

So gather your tales, let them roam,
In a wild west where laughter's a home,
With every cackle and hearty good cheer,
The dusty chronicles bring joy, oh dear!

Caravan of Memories

A caravan rolls with stories untold,
Full of mischief and laughter, quite bold,
The parrot's squawking a comic dispute,
While the ants in a line wear tiny boots.

A tumble of items spills by the road,
Old hats and mismatched shoes in a load,
With each little dingle and ding-a-ling sound,
The memories dance in a merry round.

The storyteller, sporting a grand old hat,
Shares tales of a ferret who chased after a bat,
Laughter erupts at each bend and twist,
In a rolling procession, you can't help but miss.

So pack up your bags; bring your grin,
Join the caravan where the fun begins,
With pockets of laughter and hearts all aglow,
These journeys of humor, forever will flow.

Whispers in the Breeze

The breeze brings giggles from up in the trees,
Squirrels are gossiping, sharing some cheese,
A raccoon in a mask steals a slice of pie,
As the sun winks down from the bright blue sky.

The wind carries tales of a lost rubber shoe,
Floating on air like it's something brand new,
A twist of the vine and a tickle of grass,
Whispers of fun as the moments all pass.

The gophers are dancing, each jig full of cheer,
While the owls hoot softly, sipping on beer,
It's a wild little world on this merry day,
With whispers of laughter that never decay.

So listen closely to the laughter near,
In the whispers of breezes that bring us good cheer,
In a realm of the funny where worries are few,
Where stories are spun like the sky's endless blue.

Transient Passages

In a world of quick stops and fleeting sights,
Where balloon animals take soaring flights,
A jester named Bobo rides on a kite,
Spreading his joy in the sun's warm light.

The train of giggles on a roller-coaster track,
Flops and flails bring the laughter back,
With every dip, there's a new squeaky sound,
In transient passages where fun can be found.

The clowns juggle memories like bright, shiny balls,
As the sunset paints pictures on old brick walls,
With hopscotch laughter and rhymes in the air,
They remind us all that silliness is rare.

So join in the dance, let the moments ignite,
In transient passages, our spirits take flight,
With each chuckle and smile, let joy be your task,
In the whims of the world, just cherish and bask.

Legends of the Wayward Seeds

In a field where the wild winds play,
Seeds roll around, they dance and sway.
One's gone east, another's gone west,
Searching for a home, they never rest.

A dandelion dreams of a fancy ball,
But ends up lost in a garden wall.
He wished for a partner, a puffed-up friend,
Instead, he's stuck with a cactus to tend.

Voices from the Barren Expanse

In the empty lands where shadows peek,
Lies a gossiping tumble, they squeak and speak.
One claims to have danced with a sprightly breeze,
While another just whispers about old dead trees.

Their laughter echoes beneath a scorching sun,
As they joke about journeys that never were fun.
With chuckles and snorts, they share their plight,
These seeds tell tales that stretch through the night.

The Odyssey of the Blowing Breeze

A breeze set out on a whimsical quest,
With a gust of dreams, he thought he'd be blessed.
He tickled the grasses, made flowers spin,
But got tangled in a kite stuck on a limb.

He puffed and he paused, he giggled and swirled,
Trying to impress the vast, empty world.
Yet each time he boasted of marvelous feats,
He blew away the hat from some folks on the streets.

Strands of Sunlit Solitude

On a patch of sunshine where no one would roam,
A lonely seed settled, feeling at home.
With dreams of companions, he stretched out his leaves,
But all that he got were some buzzing, bold bees.

He chuckled at clouds that drifted nearby,
Thinking, 'Perhaps I should just learn to fly!'
Yet every attempt would result in a tumble,
Making him giggle with each little jumble.

Journey of the Untamed Spirit

A tumble through the endless sand,
The spirit swirls, a sight so grand.
It skips and hops, without a care,
A playful dance through desert air.

It teases lizards in the sun,
And laughs at cactus, oh what fun!
The chase begins, a game of tag,
As tumble's laughter starts to brag.

Across the hills it rolls with glee,
A carefree soul, wild and free.
It bumps a rock, but flies right high,
Just like a kite, it hits the sky.

Oh, how it spins, in circles round,
Adventure calls—what will be found?
With every gust, new tales arise,
In dust and wind, the spirit flies.

Chronicles of the Dusty Path

A dusty trail through sunlit hay,
A jester's roll, come join the play.
It dodges boots and wanders by,
With giggles sweet beneath the sky.

Old boots complain, but who's to blame?
The little tumble moves like fame.
It spins around with joyous flair,
And tickles all, leaving them bare!

Each twist and turn, a laugh it brings,
As if it's donned a pair of wings.
Mischief weaves through every beat,
A dance of dust beneath our feet.

In every breeze, a chuckle stirs,
As merry pranks it deftly purrs.
From path to path, it carries light,
A playful breeze, a true delight.

Stories Spun by the Arid Air

The air is thick with giggles bright,
As shadows dance in fading light.
A tumble rolls past dusty news,
With tales of jest and silly blues.

It whirls around a cacti grin,
And lifts a hat from chin to chin.
The stars look down, a mocking crowd,
As laughter echoes, bold and loud.

With each new twist, a story swells,
Of cactus chats and wind-told spells.
A breeze that whispers through the land,
With every joke, the dust can stand.

Oh, hear the howls of wild delight,
As spirits dance into the night.
In arid air, the tales abound,
Of playful hearts in laughter found.

Ballads of the Restless Plains

On restless plains where laughter roams,
The tumble bounces, calling home.
It rolls through fields of golden grain,
And sings its song, a merry train.

A breeze of cheer, it weaves its tale,
As mischievous as a wily snail.
Catching whiffs of old campfire smoke,
It laughs out loud, a chorus spoke.

The sun dips low, a show begins,
A playful jig; oh, where it spins!
With every gust, a tale to tell,
In giggly notes, we laugh so well.

From dusk till dawn, the ballad plays,
As shadows dance in wild displays.
A charming round of fun we wield,
In every roll, the joy is healed.

Fables from Forgotten Canyons

In a canyon where echoes play,
A lizard danced, looking quite gay.
He wore a hat, two sizes too large,
Claimed to be the land's biggest charge.

Boulders chuckled at his wild prance,
While cacti swayed in a prickly dance.
A rabbit hopped, joining the show,
Chasing shadows, moving just so.

The wise old owl hooted a tune,
Sleepy bat bumbled by, oh so soon.
They argued over who was the star,
While the sunrise blinked from afar.

So gather 'round for a laugh or two,
These funny tales from the canyons blue.
With critters and giggles, joy never fails,
In the land of forgotten fables and tales.

The Roar of Silent Horizons

A cactus dreamed of being a tree,
Cried out, 'Why can't the world see me?'
But the wind just sighed and swirled away,
Leaving the cactus stuck in dismay.

A tumble of dust said, 'What's the fuss?'
'You'll plant your roots, and that's a must!'
The cactus nodded, swaying his spines,
Imagining branches, oh what designs!

The sun burst out, all golden and bright,
And made the horizon sparkle with light.
But the cactus remained, rooted in ground,
With laughter echoing all around.

At dusk the stars had the last word,
As crickets chirped and cats were heard.
In that land where dreams never die,
The cactus just winked at the moonlit sky.

Remnants of the Wind's Embrace

A tumble of leaves spun 'round with glee,
Met a tumblebug, quite fancy and free.
They shared a laugh at the wind's funny sway,
Dancing together 'til the end of the day.

The tumblebug said, 'I don't want to roll!'
The leaves replied with a ticklish toll.
In the gusts of laughter, they wished to remain,
Unraveling joy like an old weather vane.

But soon the sun dipped, blue turned to gray,
The wind whistled softly, urging them to play.
They tumbled and twisted in a whirlwind of cheer,
Creating a ruckus for all folk to hear.

So when you feel lost, just hear the breeze,
It carries laughter and stories with ease.
In every whisper, in each little jest,
You'll find remnants of fun that never rest.

Echoing Footsteps on Starlit Sand

On starlit sands where shadows leap,
A coyote howled, then fell in a heap.
He tripped on his tail, what a great sight,
Rolling and laughing under the night.

A tarantula wore a pair of shades,
Strutting around in sun-striped cascades.
She said, 'Fashion's important, can't you see?'
While a lizard laughed, singing out with glee.

Sneaky little mice formed a dance crew,
Shaking their tails, gathering a few.
With every step, they filled the night air,
With giggles and laughter, oh what a flair!

So if you wander the shores of the stars,
Listen for laughter, especially from Mars.
In the echo of footsteps and sandy delight,
You'll find joy dancing through the shimmering night.

Textures of a Dustbowl Dream

In a land where the wind plays games,
Dust bunnies dance with funny names.
Cacti chuckle, the sunbeam grins,
Playing tag with the tumbleweeds' spins.

The tumble of tires, a comical chase,
As cars zoom by at a laughable pace.
With each little bump, a cowboy will yell,
"Hold on tight, or you'll tumble as well!"

A prairie dog might just steal a shoe,
While a jackrabbit leaps like it's trying to flew.
The gossip of goats fills the dry air,
As they nibble on dreams without a care.

So here in this dust, we all find our cheer,
Chasing the mirage that isn't quite clear.
With laughter and love, under skies so blue,
This dusty old place is the best kind of zoo.

The Saga of Lost Highways

Down dusty trails where the road goes flat,
Seekers of fortune, dressed like a cat.
Lost like a sock in the laundry spins,
Their GPS says, "Do not drive, just grin!"

With gas stations closed and snacks well past due,
They barter with coyotes for a wild brew.
Lizards give directions with a sly little wink,
While cows ponder life on the edge of the brink.

Riding in trucks that squeak and whine,
Each mile a story, each turn a sign.
A flat tire somehow turns into a dance,
With a boogie-woogie, they take a chance.

So here in the wild, where laughter can roam,
Lost highways lead us to a comical home.
With quirks and a shrug, let the journey unfold,
For the tales that we weave are worth more than gold.

A Journey Beyond the Dust Clouds

When dust clouds gather, and storms start to swirl,
Adventurers chuckle and give a twirl.
With wind in their hair and grit on their cheeks,
They dream about treasures and comical peaks.

With donkeys and mules, they hit the old trails,
Trading tall tales about wagon wheel fails.
Each bump in the road brings laughter anew,
As they dodge tumbleweeds, like crazy fools do.

Sitting 'round fires, exchanging wild lore,
A skunk named McGuffin becomes legendary more.
With s'mores and bad jokes, the night ends in glee,
As stars wink above, and they sing off-key.

In the heart of the dust, funny stories unfold,
Where laughter's the treasure, and memories gold.
So join in the fun, let your spirit be free,
For the journey is sweeter than it seems to be.

Shadows Wandering in the Wilderness

The shadows stretch long in the evening light,
While creatures of mirth start to take flight.
With squirrels on scooters and owls with cool shades,
The wilderness giggles, their escapades made.

A raccoon with glasses reads maps upside down,
While a rabbit wears sneakers, king of the town.
As shadows prance lightly, they embroider the night,
With a chorus of chuckles, a comical sight.

Beneath buzzing stars, a coyote hums tunes,
While critters join in, howling with loons.
With shadows a-dancing, the laughter runs deep,
In the wilderness, joy creates stories to keep.

So here in the wild, let the mingling begin,
With echoes of laughter, as wild as the wind.
The shadows may wander, but fun's never far,
For the wilderness knows just who we are.

Mystique of the Wind-Worn Trails

On dusty paths where critters play,
A hat can fly, then roll away.
The jackrabbit hops, a sight so grand,
While tumbleweed winks, holding its stand.

A cactus chuckles, spikes in tow,
As the curious breeze begins to blow.
A wandering sock finds its own parade,
In this comical journey 'neath sun and shade.

The Dance of the Eroding Hills

Atop the hills, the roosters crow,
While rocks roll down, putting on a show.
A squirrel slips, does a tiny flip,
In this wacky world, no chance to trip.

The dust bunnies whirl, in giggles they spin,
As tumble tumble weeds join in the din.
The breeze is a clown, tickling our nose,
Here in the land where silliness grows.

Trails of the Whispering Wilderness

Through branches sway the tales so sly,
With echoing laughter as they pass by.
A lost shoe chuckles, in bushes it hides,
As the moonlight giggles, it softly collides.

The critters chatter in whispers and grins,
Spinning their stories, with giggly wins.
An owl hoots tune, a jazz beat in play,
Under the stars, in this funny ballet.

The Saga of Solitary Sands

In a desert where the shadows pop,
A lone tumble has a lonesome bop.
A fancy hat flies, declaring its fate,
With each little flip, it's never too late.

Cacti watch closely, with prickly cheer,
While a sand dune dreams of a dance so near.
Laughter erupts in this sandy expanse,
As laughter and giggles break into a dance.

A Whisper from the Wandering Earth

A tumble and a twist in the breeze,
A sock got lost, oh such a tease!
Round and round, it spins with glee,
Rescue it? Nah, let it be free.

The cactus waved hello quite high,
While squirrels danced beneath the sky,
A tumble here, a spin, a roll,
Nature's jesters, oh what a stroll!

The rocks chuckled, they know the game,
While I chase shadows, feeling quite lame,
Who knew the earth could be so sly?
Running in circles, oh me, oh my!

So here I am, two left feet,
With nature's giggles, can't face defeat,
But in this dance, I'll always partake,
Laughter's the treasure, make no mistake!

Dreams in the Dunes of Time

In the desert, I lost my hat,
It flew on by like a playful cat,
Chasing it down seemed so absurd,
Like following dreams that flit and blurt.

The sand whispered tales of ancient fun,
Of mirages dancing under the sun,
While I tripped over cactus so grand,
Just my luck, how odd, how unplanned!

A lizard laughed, as I took a tumble,
Into a pile of prickly jumble,
But oh, my pride was firmly intact,
Crafting laughs with each little act!

So here's to the sun and the dunes' sweet sway,
Each step a story, who could dismay?
With giggles trapped in the grains of sand,
I'll dance through this desert, as laughter's the plan!

Ballad of the Nomadic Heart

With a beat-up truck and dreams so wide,
I roam the roads, with joy as my guide,
The cows look on with a bemused stare,
As I sing my songs into the air.

Where to next? Not quite sure,
Life's a buffet, and I want more,
Each town I pass, a tale to unfold,
Of mischief and mishaps, never old!

A map's a guide, but laughter's my fate,
I'll stop for coffee, maybe a plate,
And with each chuckle, my heart feels light,
In the journey of life, I find delight!

So here's to the roads that lead me free,
With every twist, a new comedy,
No destination, just wander and play,
Nomadic heart, dancing the day away!

The Song of the Sunlit Outback

In the sunlit outback, oh what a sight,
A kangaroo hops, it takes flight!
My drink spills over, what a disgrace,
But laughter erupts, can't hide my face.

The emus strut, and so do I,
With a waddle and giggle, oh my, oh my!
The dusty road sings a jolly tune,
Beneath the watchful eye of the moon.

A picnic planned, but ants took the feast,
They marched with pride, the pesky beast!
I waved them off, but they danced with glee,
Such a funny mess, just let it be!

So here in the outback, I find my cheer,
With mishaps and laughter, nothing to fear,
For every stumble is a dance step, true,
In this sunny land where the laughter grew!

Notes from the Wind's Journey

A tumble and a twist, oh what a sight,
The wind plays tricks in the soft twilight.
With whispers and giggles, it dances around,
Picking up laughter from the dusty ground.

It scoops up a shoe, and a hat flies high,
Chasing a cat that is questioning why.
The trees all chuckle, they bend and sway,
As the wind takes off for another wild play.

Reveries of the Rolling Sand

In the dunes, they tumble, restless and free,
Rolling together, oh what glee!
A scattered adventure, quite absurd,
Chasing the sun, not a single word.

Sand on a mission, never quite still,
Finding new places, a glittering thrill.
A festival of grains under the blue,
Plotting a dance, just me and you.

Myths of the Mysterious Waste

Once in a desert, so hot and wide,
Lived a cactus with pride, it just couldn't hide.
A tale of shenanigans it surely told,
Of friendships with rocks that grew fearless and bold.

The lizards would listen as sunbeams sing,
Hatching up plans for the next big fling.
Oh, the stories they spun in the sandy domain,
Myths told of mischief, a whimsical gain.

The Unraveled Tale of Nature's Stray

A hapless leaf danced from tree to tree,
Giggling and spinning, just wild and free.
It rolled past a mole with a curious stare,
Saying, 'Join me, friend, on a breeze (if you dare)!'

With each twist and turn, oh what a sight,
The leaf led a parade into the night.
A wacky escapade, a drift and a sway,
Nature's own circus, in a playful display.

Cantos of the Sun-Scorched Earth

Baked by the sun, the ground does frown,
Gritty laughter rolls, it tumbles down.
Cacti dance, with arms outstretched,
Whistling tunes, in silence fetched.

From rocks to weeds, they start their cheer,
A mirage of jokes floats, oh so near.
Sunburnt grins wave in the heat,
Found some shade? Well, isn't that sweet!

Dry gusts sing like a rusty band,
Spinning wild tales across the land.
But if you listen close, you'll find,
The secrets of a laughing mind.

Each crack in the earth, a jest concealed,
Tales of the drought, the drought revealed.
So let your spirit dance and swirl,
In this sun-baked, mirth-filled whirl.

Voices of the Blissful Breeze

Whispers of wind, a cheeky affair,
Tickling the trees, with wavy hair.
Leaves chuckle softly, as they flip,
While butterflies take their funny trip.

Onward they float, the breeze does tease,
Frolicking amongst the dancing leaves.
With every gust, a playful jest,
Nature's comedy, at its best.

Clouds roll by, with a wink or two,
Casting shadows of laughter anew.
A giggle escapes from the clouds so bright,
As day turns to dusk, under starry light.

With every breeze, a tale is spun,
A chorus of joy, that's never done.
So lean in close, and take a ride,
On the laughter of the turning tide.

The Flight of the Wind-Kissed Grass

Dewy blades play, a wiggly dance,
Inviting the daisies to join in the prance.
A breeze pulls them low, then up they soar,
Like grasshoppers high, on nature's floor.

Grass whispers secrets, in rustling tones,
Telling tall tales to the skimming stones.
With every wiggle, a giggling wave,
An enchanting chorus, wild and brave.

Little critters march, their own parade,
In the arms of the grass, they've made their trade.
Shadows of laughter ripple and leap,
In this ongoing jest, where we all can peek.

So hop with the grass, let your worries go,
Ride the wind's giggles, join the show.
In every sway, a new jest lies,
Beneath the big, starry skies.

Harmony of the Dusty Ballad

Dust clouds forming, a merry old twist,
On roads less traveled, you can't resist.
Chasing the dirt, like a playful ghost,
In this dusty ballad, we laugh the most.

With each tumble and tumble, giggles arise,
The sun paints the scene; oh what a surprise!
Gravelly grins flirt with the breeze,
While ants do the tango, with utmost ease.

In the shadows of hills, odd stories blend,
With rattling laughter, as creatures descend.
They burst into song, a clattering tune,
Under the glow of a mischievous moon.

So join the parade of the dust and mirth,
A riot of whimsy, a celebration of earth.
In every grain, a chuckle is found,
In this playful symphony, joy abounds.

Wandering Spirits

In the desert's dry embrace,
A cowboy lost his shoe,
Chasing whispers on the breeze,
He spun and danced, quite a view!

Lizards laughed and joined the fun,
As cacti rolled their eyes,
A tumble down the sandy hill,
Brought forth a surprise.

A jackrabbit with a grin,
Took that shoe and made a home,
Now he wears it every day,
A fashionable roaming gnome!

The spirits of the sands laugh loud,
At antics of the past,
In this land where mirth abounds,
The good times hold steadfast.

Rustling Reveries

A gust of wind, a dancing leaf,
Twisted tales of woe,
A ghostly drum, a chuckling tune,
It's a lively desert show.

The rattlesnake strums its notes,
While the tumbleweed plays the part,
A band of desert misfits join,
Their laughter fills the heart.

Cactus stands in mock surprise,
At this baffling parade,
With everyone in on the joke,
They jump and jive unafraid.

Underneath that burning sun,
A headliner rolls on through,
The spirits dance till dusk arrives,
These antics never rue.

Desert Chronicles

Once a lizard took a trip,
On a skateboard made of sand,
Rolling down the twisted trails,
Leaving footprints oh so grand.

Tumbleweeds formed a crowd,
Cheering him with rattled glee,
While tumblebugs tried to race,
But they were all too buzzy, see?

In the shade of ancient rocks,
A hero's welcome came around,
The lizard's fame was short-lived,
For he fell, and then rolled down!

With laughter echoed through the dunes,
The desert shared a grin,
Tomorrow brings another tale,
Let the shenanigans begin!

Ashen Skylines

A lone crow flew overhead,
An artist in disguise,
Painting shadows on the sand,
With mischief in its eyes.

An old rancher's hat took flight,
Riding on a playful breeze,
It twirled and dipped, a merry sight,
As if to dance with trees.

The horizon split in giggles bright,
As tumbleweed spun like a top,
A twirling show beneath the sun,
In this zany desert shop.

With every gust that blows about,
A story finds its way,
The skyline echoes with their laughs,
As night turns into day.

Driftwood Dreams Beneath the Stars

In a driftwood chair, I take my rest,
Stars twinkle above, each one a jest.
A crab scuttles by, surely in a race,
While I sip my drink, with a grin on my face.

The sea whispers tales of sailors long gone,
While I ponder why I left my lawn.
The waves pull a sock from my beach bag near,
I realize then, my mind's not quite clear.

The surf shouts its riddle with a salty cheer,
As I laugh at a seagull that swoops in near.
It's a mishmash of dreams, drifting east and west,
In this woodsy chair, I feel truly blessed.

So here's to the driftwood, a cozy old friend,
With its quips and its quirks that never seem to end.
I raise up my glass to the antics of fate,
For laughter and dreams, it's never too late.

Puzzles of the Parched Landscape

The desert's a puzzle, a wacky old game,
With cacti who dance, though they're all the same.
A lizard named Frank, with a top hat so grand,
Claims he's the ruler of this dusty land.

The sun plays the jester, with warmth that's absurd,
While shadows of tumbleweeds whisper unheard.
A tumble by chance, but no one will tell,
The humor in nature, it's working so well.

With footprints just trailing where no one has gone,
A mirage offers ice cream, but it's just a con.
The wind tries to tickle the sand on my toes,
As questions of logic swirl where no one knows.

So here's to the mysteries, the giggles, the strife,
In a land where the odd becomes part of life.
Where each grain of sand tells a story, you see,
And every old cactus winks back at me.

Memories of the Grassy Mirage

In fields that are green, my mind starts to sway,
Where grass seems to giggle and dance in the play.
A rabbit named Monty with spectacles round,
Claims he's the wisest in this bouncy ground.

The daisies are gossiping, sharing a laugh,
While butterflies flitter like pages in half.
A breeze gives a nudge, whispers charms in my ear,
As I wonder if daisies drink root beer here.

Each blade a comedian, each story a jest,
In this mirage of memories, I feel truly blessed.
With laughter that echoes through wildflower fields,
And the secrets of nature, humor reveals.

So dance with the daisies, take part in the fun,
Join Monty the rabbit, let's all be one.
For life's just a tapestry woven with dreams,
Where laughter is shining, and nothing's as it seems.

The Enigma of Endless Roads

Each road is an enigma, a winding old friend,
With twists and with turns that seem never to end.
A signpost that giggles, asking "Where to now?"
While clouds above look on, with a coy little bow.

The pavement's a storyteller, spills tales on the way,
Of hitchhikers jiving with quirky ballet.
With a cactus that grins and a lizard that sings,
These roads bring the laughter that adventure brings.

I meet a lost sock on the shoulder ahead,
It winks as I pass; is it seeking a bed?
A tumble of laughter rolls under my feet,
While crickets provide the rhythm, the beat.

So let's journey together, with mirth as our guide,
In this wacky world, where the silly abide.
Every twist in the road unveils something bright,
In the enigma of travel, there's no end to delight.

Wanderlust Whispers

On a breeze that carries cheer,
A restless seed has found its sphere.
It rolls and tumbles with delight,
Chasing shadows, out of sight.

With every bound, it tells a joke,
Of bumbling critters, and silly folk.
It spins around like a carefree sprite,
In the golden sun, so warm and bright.

It winks at clouds, as it moves along,
Singing softly a funny song.
Each twist and turn, a comic dance,
A journey bold, a wild romance.

Alas, it stops near a cactus grin,
Buried in laughter, it rolls again.
For life is short, a jolly ride,
With whispers loud, and nothing to hide.

Dances of the Dust

In a patch of sun, the dust does sway,
As secrets float from day to day.
Each speck a dancer, spry and free,
Twisting about, just wait and see.

They gather in circles, a merry band,
Spinning together, hand in hand.
They giggle and choke, in a pirouette,
Leaving behind a cloud so wet.

A fancy waltz under a rusty moon,
Making all who linger laugh and swoon.
In silly formation, across the plain,
Dust bunnies bounce in a carefree chain.

When winds come howling, they fly away,
A fleeting encore to end the play.
With a final twirl, they embrace the sky,
Leaving behind tales that flutter and fly.

Ephemeral Echoes

A rolling stone goes on its way,
Chasing laughter at the end of the day.
It gathers tales from here and there,
Whispers of joy float high in the air.

Under a bright and twinkling star,
It shares a yarn from places afar.
Funny mishaps of friends it meets,
In a world of chuckles, where laughter greets.

Through laughter, it winds like a kite,
Spreading stories that tickle the night.
It peeks at the moon with a cheeky grin,
Celebrating life with each silly spin.

And as dawn breaks, it fades from view,
Leaving behind giggles, fresh as the dew.
An echo of joy that swiftly flows,
In the time of the wind, anything goes.

Stories on the Wind

The wind has tales spun fine as thread,
Whimsical moments that bounce in your head.
From jester's hats to frogs in boots,
In this wild world, anything suits.

It whistles a tune of a far-off land,
Where llamas dance and do the fandango grand.
Across the fields, each story twirls,
In merry spins, their laughter unfurls.

Among the tumble of leaves and dust,
A narrative leaps, it's full of lust.
With each gust, more giggles arise,
As it kisses cheeks under sunlit skies.

When the dusk arrives with a wink so sly,
The stories linger, they never die.
For laughter is the song of the breeze,
That carries joy through each rustling tease.

Echoes of the Forgotten Frontier

In the land where squirrels plot,
Cactus jigs by the old dusty lot,
A cowboy's hat flew with a shout,
Chasing tumblebugs, what a rout!

A horse named Bingo lost his shoes,
Rodeo clowns with no real clues,
Hitching their wagons to a star,
Singing songs of a near-mythical car.

With every gust, tall tales arise,
Lizards wear hats, much to our surprise,
Flicks of laughter dance in the breeze,
As tumbleweeds tease with mischievous ease.

Their secrets shared in the wild moonlight,
Where Jackalopes dance and the owls take flight,
In this frontier, where oddballs convene,
Life's a hoot in the bright silver sheen!

Adventures Beneath the Infinite Sky

Under a canvas of endless cheer,
Dancing cacti uphold their career,
A roadrunner bursts into a race,
Chasing a tumbling hat with such grace.

Clouds play hide and seek on high,
While tumblebugs dream of learning to fly,
A lizard named Lou prances about,
Spinning tales of what life's all about.

With campfires crackling and stars aglow,
A quirky band of critters in tow,
Singing nonsense to the tune of a breeze,
Tickling our souls with teasing degrees.

Laughter and joy bubble up like spring,
As coyotes yowl, oh what joy they bring,
Under this vast and silly display,
Adventures unfold in the quirkiest way!

Chronicles of the Nomad's Heart

A wandering soul with a whimsy oath,
Roaming the plains since he took an oath,
With a pack full of snacks, he counts each mile,
And chuckles at cacti that seem to smile.

Doc the turtle, slow but spry,
Dreams of racing - Oh my, oh my!
While tumbleweed scouts make their rounds,
Reporting on wanderers with laughter profound.

Every campfire tells a silly tale,
Of floppy eared bunnies and a brave snail,
Ghost stories told with a wink and a grin,
In this nomadic life where fun's always in.

With the sunset painting absurdity bright,
They dance in the dark from dusk until light,
Chasing dreams with a heartbeat so bold,
In these chronicles, laughter unfolds!

Whirlwinds of Memory and Dust

In a town that forgot how to frown,
Old Bob spins tales of a lost golden crown,
With each whirlwind, memories dust off,
As tumbleweed laughs, it just can't scoff.

Sandy shoes and a kaleidoscope hat,
A raccoon debates whether he's a cat,
Pinecones gossip while the sun shines down,
Crafting stories that dance in the town.

Down the main street, where giggles ignite,
Stray cats duel in a comical fight,
A juggler arrives, he's quite the sight,
With pins that are bathed in starlit delight.

Yet through the chaos, the joy flows free,
As dusty wind whispers, "Come laugh with me,"
In whirlwinds of time that spin and twirl,
Life's a funny puzzle, a wild swirl!

Tales of the Open Range

A cactus learned to dance with glee,
But tripped and fell, oh poor, poor Lee.
The tumble down was quite the sight,
As laughter echoed through the night.

A cowboy's hat took off in flight,
It soared like dreams into the night.
The horses laughed, they rolled in dirt,
While cowboys yelled, "Hey, watch that shirt!"

A jackrabbit wore a bowtie neat,
Declared a glamor contest, quite sweet.
But when he hopped, it caused a fuss,
The other critters rode the bus.

An old coyote sang a song,
In melodies that felt so wrong.
The sheep all baaa-ed with joyful cheer,
While owls whooped, "What a premiere!"

Cirrus of the Forsaken

A cloud thought it could puff and strut,
Wound up wedged in a old barn's rut.
The cows looked up, in pure dismay,
And whispered, "That's no cloud today!"

A breeze decided to play a prank,
Tickling trees from the left flank.
It shook the leaves, they fell in heaps,
The squirrels squeaked, "We'll lose our keeps!"

A lizard lost his brave disguise,
When caught beneath the moonlit skies.
He blushed, turned green, then turned to flee,
While crickets chirped, "That's not so free!"

The stars conspired to make a wish,
But forgot to get their midnight dish.
So all they did was blink and glow,
As dreams rolled in, just like a show!

Whispers of the Wandering Dust

A tumbleweed held court on a mound,
Declared its reign, then spun around.
Dust bunnies giggled, full of mirth,
As party hats rolled down to earth.

An old boot claimed it was a shoe,
But lost its sole, it just won't do.
The rusting fence teased and whirred,
"Come join the game, you silly bird!"

A lizard in a bandana stood,
Singing tunes from his brotherhood.
The rabbits danced, the hawks just stared,
While the cactus laughed, "He hasn't cared!"

The moon peeked down, with a wink and nod,
"Keep that ruckus up; it feels quite odd!"
The night carried tales through the space,
Of dusty roads and a silly chase!

Echoes of the Desert Wind

A saguaro tried a new hairstyle,
With pom-poms stuck, it looked quite vile.
The owls hooted, unable to cope,
"Stop that nonsense, we want some hope!"

A dance-off happened, just see that feat,
Between a gopher and a shy fleet.
They twirled and tumbled, fell on their backs,
While the tortoise cheered, "Well, that's no act!"

A rattler rattled his way to fame,
Said, "Watch me hiss, I'll play this game!"
But got tangled in a cactus' spines,
And squeaked, "Now I'm in quite the bind!"

The wind just laughed and swirled around,
Picking up giggles from the ground.
It carried all those funny notes,
Through desert dreams on silent boats!

Secrets Within the Scrublands

In the dry lands where whispers conspire,
Lies an old tale that never grows tired.
A critter scurries, a hidden surprise,
With secrets tucked under the starry skies.

Cacti giggle while crickets debate,
Who'll be the first to cook up fate?
The lizards chat, in coats of green hue,
Planning mischief, just for a few.

Scorpions dance with their shadows at play,
While jackrabbits hop, never in dismay.
Each brush hides a laugh, a chuckle or two,
In the scrublands where the wild things grew.

Oh, the desert's alive with tricks, loads of fun,
In the scent of sagebrush, adventures begun.
So come take a stroll through the wild, oh so bold,
And laugh at the stories that never grow old.

Serenade of the Wandering Skies

Clouds float by, like drifting balloons,
While the sun hums along to the afternoon tunes.
A kite caught in laughter twirls and spins,
Chasing the breeze, where the adventure begins.

Birds gossip loudly, trading their news,
While the wind sways the wildflower hues.
The turtles are plotting a race with the breeze,
As the crows croon songs that tickle with ease.

Raindrops are jesters, with dances so spry,
Tickling the rooftops low in the sky.
Each flash of lightning creates quite a scene,
Oh, who knew weather could be so keen?

With each puffy cloud and each ray of light,
Nature's orchestra plays into the night.
And as stars twinkle, the stories unfold,
Of skies ever wandering, forever bold.

Threads of a Dusty Narrative

A lonely sock rolls down a dirt track,
Mismatched companions, no turning back.
The tumble of tales from each dusty shoe,
Whisper of journeys where few ever flew.

Dandelions giggle in a cloudy parade,
While tumblebugs lead a quirky charade.
Each whispering breeze carries distant lore,
Of dust that remembers, forevermore.

A mischievous breeze sends old tales afloat,
On the back of a snail riding a boat.
The gravel sings softly a song of delight,
As stories of wanderers dance in the night.

So gather your tales, let the stories unroll,
For the world loves a laugh, it brings joy to the soul.
In the rhythm of dust, let your spirit ignite,
As we spin every tale until morning light.

The Unknown Journey of a Leaf

Once a proud leaf on a tall, sturdy oak,
Decided one day, it was tired of smoke.
With a gusty goodbye, it waved to the branch,
Setting off on a whimsical chance.

In the crisp autumn air, it danced with glee,
Swirling around, oh what a sight to see!
It rolled with a tumble, got stuck in a fence,
Wondering why it ever felt so intense.

A squirrel gave chase, thinking it a snack,
But the leaf just chuckled and slipped through a crack.
On a journey so wild, with nothing to fear,
Finding new friends, and laughter sincere.

So off flew the leaf, on a breeze so sweet,
Riding the winds with the dust at its feet.
In the circle of life, it twirls and it spins,
Leaving behind a trail of grins.

Nomadic Dreams

In the desert dance, I twirl and spin,
Chasing my hat, oh, where to begin?
With dust in my eyes and a grin on my face,
I wander around like I own this place.

Cacti are friends, they never complain,
They stand there tall, while I feel the strain.
My shoes are all dusty, I tripped on a rock,
Yet here I am laughing, tick-tock, tick-tock.

The tumble in tumbleweeds is rather quite bold,
They tumble on past, a sight to behold.
I try to keep up, but my legs are all sore,
And each little tumble makes me love them more.

So let's share a jest, if we can get along,
We'll spin 'round the campfire, laugh all night long.
In a world that's so wild, let's throw up our hands,
For nomadic dreams, and silly, sweet bands.

Solitary Journeys

On roads less traveled, where whispers reside,
I ride on my bike with no one beside.
The wind plays my tune, a funny old song,
While I dodge tumbleweeds, hopping along.

With snacks in my pocket, I'm ready to roam,
In search of the best, just a little bit far from home.
My map is the sky, with clouds for my guide,
I'll get lost in the laughter and leave doubts inside.

A squirrel with a mustache crosses my path,
I burst out in giggles, I can't help but laugh.
Each turn is a giggle and with every new sight,
My solitary journey is feeling just right.

So if you see me, please don't be shy,
Join in on the fun, let's let laughter fly.
For solitary paths can turn quite absurd,
Just two wanderers sharing the unheard.

Restless Seeds

Seeds in the breeze, dance with delight,
Rolling along in the warm morning light.
They tumble and jiggle, each twist a delight,
Like little green jesters, they take off in flight.

I once met a seed who thought he could sprout,
He claimed he was special, no room for doubt.
But he rolled off a cliff with a laugh and a spin,
And landed in dirt with a sheepish grin.

They gather in corners, they plot and they scheme,
"What if we sprout in a wacky dream?"
With roots in the air and leaves in the mud,
These restless seed buddies just want to feel good.

So here's to the seeds, with their jovial plays,
In fields filled with laughter, let's cherish their ways.
For life is a tumble, a dance we can lead,
Let's laugh like the flowers and follow that seed!

Chasing Shadows

A shadow runs quick, I'm giving a chase,
It giggles and hides, oh what a race!
In a wacky world of mismatched light,
I chase after shapes through the day and the night.

A cat crossed my path, it sat in a pose,
Its shadow grew long, and I struck a quick nose.
The cat just meowed and gave me a sigh,
As if to suggest, "Oh why even try?"

The sun plays tricks, with giggles and glee,
Creating odd shapes, just for me.
With every new turn, I tumble and fall,
Just a jester in sunlight, laughing with all.

So join in the fun, don't let shadows slack,
Let's dance in the light and never look back.
For shadows can play too, a game that's divine,
Chasing after laughter, it's just so sublime!

Songs of the Scattered

In the winds we dance, oh what a sight,
Chasing our hats on a wild and bright night.
A swirl and a twirl, we tumble and roll,
Laughing together, we're out of control.

A rabbit hops by, with a top hat askew,
He tips his cap kindly, as if he just knew.
With shoes made of clouds, and socks full of cheer,
We twirl and we spin, with nothing to fear.

The cactus is laughing, it pokes at the sun,
'Hey, come join the party! We're just having fun!'
With drinks made of wishes, and chips from the sky,
We parties till midnight, oh me, oh my!

So gather your friends, let's chase after fate,
In the winds, we find joy—a merry old state.
For scattered we are, like leaves in the breeze,
But laughter connects us, oh how it does please!

Fables of the Forgotten

In a land that once buzzed, where stories lay still,
A frog in a waistcoat, with hope for a thrill.
He croaks old tales of the days that are past,
With a wink and a hop, he makes laughs that last.

A sleepy old tortoise, with glasses on tight,
Claims the moon was a cheese wheel, oh what a sight!
He speaks with such wisdom, but always a grin,
When asked for his secret, he just winks and spins.

The myths fade away, like dust on the floor,
But giggles and chuckles still linger at the door.
A bear brings the honey, the bees sing along,
And suddenly forgotten is where we belong.

So let's spin anew, with the tale we create,
In the land of the silly, we celebrate fate.
For laughter's the treasure, the memories gold,
In fables of joy, we'll never grow old.

Embrace of the Elements

The sun sets in laughter, as clouds start to play,
They tickle the ground, and the grass joins the fray.
In puddles we splash, like kids on a spree,
Rain boots hitting water, oh what glee!

A breeze with a chuckle, it zips through the trees,
Whispering secrets and rustling the leaves.
It twirls round our ankles and lifts up our hats,
With a spin and a laugh, we're all acrobats!

The moon joins the fun, with a wink and a grin,
It plays peek-a-boo, past a toothy old tin.
The stars wink above, like they're part of the show,
While crickets play tunes that we all love to know.

So gather your friends, let's revel and roam,
With elements' joy, we create a home.
In this funny embrace, the world bursts with light,
Where laughter's the heartbeat, from morning to night.

Wayfarer's Journals

A traveler stumbles, with shoes far too big,
He trips on a pebble, falls down with a jig.
His compass is spinning, but laughter is true,
He maps out his journey with giggles askew.

He faces the mountains, with dreams like bright kites,
Eagles swoop down, sharing curious sights.
'Hey, up in the sky, could you lend me a wing?'
They chuckle and circle, 'let's see what you bring.'

Through valleys of chuckles and fields of good cheer,
This wanderer wanders, with nothing to fear.
He scribbles on parchment the jokes that he hears,
With doodles of llamas and silly old fears.

So pen down your tales, let laughter take flight,
With friends by your side, every day's pure delight.
For in the wayfarer's heart, joy never departs,
As he journeys through life, it's the laughter that starts.

Driftwood Diaries

In the sun, a log did dance,
A twist and turn, it took a chance.
A seagull laughed, it took the lead,
While driftwood swayed with gentle speed.

The tide would rise, and then it'd fall,
Resting near the beach's call.
With every wave, it told a joke,
A sunburned shell chased it, bespoke.

Together they would ride the swell,
Sharing stories, oh so well.
A fish gasped in disbelief,
As laughter burst like ocean grief.

And when the night began to loom,
The driftwood grinned, defying gloom.
Stars winked bright, the moon's delight,
A million stories by the light.

Whirling Stories

A tumble in the sandy breeze,
A tumbleweed, with such a tease.
It rolls and spins with cheeky glee,
Whispering tales of wild esprit.

A cowboy stops with hat in hand,
To hear the tales from this strange land.
He chuckles low, as it rolls past,
A funny friend, so free and fast.

A lizard claims it for a throne,
While chuckling at the seeds it's sown.
A cactus joins in, oh what a sight,
Two prickly pals, both laughing bright.

As sunset paints the world in gold,
The stories shared are tales retold.
Through winds so wild, they find their way,
To bring some joy to every day.

Echoes of the Open Road

A vintage car with squeaks and creaks,
Makes friends with dust, as it sneaks.
With each bump, it sings a tune,
Echoed laughter under the moon.

The road stretched out, a ribbon wide,
Adventure calls, come join the ride.
A raccoon waves from a tree nearby,
While passing clouds just wave and sigh.

Travelers pose with cheesy grins,
As signs proclaim their silly wins.
With burgers stacked, the stories flowed,
Each bite a laugh on this long road.

The sunset painted skies so grand,
As echoes whisper, take my hand.
With every mile, the heart would soar,
Each laugh a memory, wanting more.

Sagebrush Serenade

In sagebrush fields where crickets sing,
A serenade from nature's fling.
A rabbit hops, then trips with flair,
While laughing at the absent air.

A lizard posed like it could dance,
In wild defiance, took a chance.
Where tumblebugs rolled in delight,
Their mini parades spark silly sight.

A punchy breeze, it sneezes loud,
As if the sagebrush formed a crowd.
With every rustle, giggles spread,
A comedy show, all green and red.

Beneath the stars, they gathered tight,
To swap their tales and end the night.
With every whisper, every cheer,
The sagebrush sang, oh so sincere.

Stories from the Edge of Nowhere

In a town where whispers play,
A cactus wore a hat today.
It danced to songs of wind and sand,
While folks just shook their heads and planned.

A lizard leaped and stole some fries,
Claimed he was a king in disguise.
The diner laughed, the jukebox roared,
As tumbleweeds drifted, feeling bored.

The sheriff chased a ghostly cow,
Who dared to poke its head in now.
The jokes they shared with each pursuit,
Made every day a funny hoot.

A postcard sent from nowhere fair,
With scribbles and a pie in air.
We'll laugh as long as stars align,
In this place where odd tales intertwine.

Lament of the Dusty Traveler

Oh, the roads that twist and curl,
With tumbleweeds that spin and twirl.
A traveler lost his map one night,
Found only cacti to hold him tight.

He sneezed at dust, a mighty sound,
And startled everyone around.
A sparrow giggled on a wire,
While dreaming dreams of fluffy pies for hire.

He wore a coat of faded dreams,
With pockets stuffed with crazy schemes.
The sun grinned wide on weary plains,
As laughter danced through joyful chains.

Yet in the end, he found his way,
Through silliness that ruled the day.
In every bend, a story's spun,
Leaving joy, instead of fun undone.

Sunlit Chronicles on the Horizon

Under bright skies, the sun did gleam,
A sassy squirrel hatched a dream.
He planned a party, wild and loud,
    Inviting every creature proud.

A rabbit hopped, wearing a suit,
Declared it time for carrots and fruit.
The dance floor made from golden hay,
    Became the hit of the sunny day.

As shadows lengthened, mirth took flight,
From buzzing bees, a sweet delight.
They painted skies with wild delight,
As giggles rang through the starry night.

With every tale from dusk till dawn,
The whispers of fun lingered on.
Here on this horizon wide,
    Laughter, joy, and magic bide.

The Wanderlust of the Forgotten

A dusty road where dreams collide,
With stories waiting to abide.
An old man strummed his heart away,
While children danced, all bright and gay.

He spoke of towns that lost their name,
Where folks forgot the rules of fame.
Yet every face he proudly met,
Joined in the fun without regret.

They built a castle made of sand,
With towers leaning, not so grand.
A seagull stole a tattered crown,
Proclaiming laughter as the town's renown.

Though never found on any map,
This place awoke when dreams overlap.
In wanderlust, they forged their fate,
A funny land, where joy won great.

Shadows of the Roaming Sage

In a town where the sun likes to bake,
A sage tried to dance, for goodness' sake.
He twirled with the dust, and kicked up a plume,
But a cactus remarked, "You've sealed your own doom!"

He hopped on a cart with a cat and a dog,
Said, "Let's chase some clouds!" They laughed like a fog.

But the wagon wheel squeaked, like a duck on a whim,
And the sage sang a tune, though it sounded quite grim.

One day he found fortune in an old rusty shoe,
Proclaimed, "From this moment, I'm rich!"—Oh, if he knew.
For the shoe held a rat that just wanted a nap,
And it jumped out and scurried, escaping the trap!

At last, he sat down by the cracked canyon wall,
With a grin on his face, he dismissed it all.
As shadows danced with a mischievous glee,
The sage laughed aloud, 'This is better than tea!'

Memoirs of the Forsaken Trail

On a forsaken trail where the tumblebugs roam,
Lived a coyote named Carl who wanted a home.
He gathered his friends, a wise old jackrabbit,
And told them his dream, oh, they thought he was mad!

With a map made of leaves and a compass of twine,
They set off through the bushes, oh what a fine line!
But every direction led them in circles,
They once met a lizard who danced in his swirls.

"Where's the prize?" Carl barked, with a quirk in his grin,

As the lizard replied, "You forgot where to begin!"
In a whirlwind of laughter, they spun on the ground,
With a rattle and clap, they jumped up with a bound.

When the sun set ablaze, the trip seemed just right,
For in every wrong turn, they found delight.
With tales to tell under the starry night's veil,
They chuckled together, the best kind of trail!

The Last Dance of the Rolling Grass

There once grew some grass with a party to throw,
It invited the winds, the critters, the show.
With a twist and a twirl, it shimmied with cheer,
Proclaiming aloud, "We're the best dancers here!"

But a squirrel named Sammy was feeling left out,
He danced on a branch, and he started to shout.
"Hey, you leafy show-offs, just wait till I'm done!"
And he launched from the tree in a leap full of fun.

Down he plopped in a tumble, oh what a scene,
A flip in the air till he landed pristine!
The grass cheered him on, with a rustling cheer,
And they giggled together, as if it were clear.

Then the breeze blew a tune that made grasses sway,
And the friends spun around, making merry all day.
With the sun in the sky, and their spirits so high,
They danced till the stars were a blanket on high!

Secrets Carried on the Breeze

There once was a whisper that roamed in the air,
It tickled the ears of a curious bear.
"What's that?" he asked as it flitted around,
But all that he heard was a giggly sound.

The breeze played a game, telling secrets galore,
Of a turtle who dreamed of becoming a chore.
He wanted to dance, but his shell was too wide,
Still, he practiced each move with a bounce and a pride.

Then came a wise owl, perched high in a tree,
"Dear turtle, just try, it's as easy as three!"
So, he shuffled and tumbled, out under the moon,
With the breeze as his partner, they danced to a tune.

They worked up a rhythm, a jive in the night,
As the stars twinkled down, sparking joy and delight.
And as dawn peeked through, the secrets were shed,
For the bear just could chuckle at the things that he said!

www.ingramcontent.com/pod-product-compliance
Lightning Source LLC
Chambersburg PA
CBHW071838160426
43209CB00003B/338